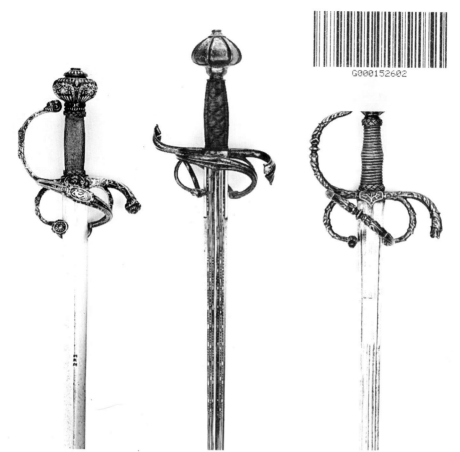

(Left to right) Italian rapier with urn-shaped pommel, decorated with a female nude on the loop guard, c.1560; Italian rapier, c.1600, with pierced blade of German manufacture; German rapier bearing patriotic inscriptions and the medallion of the elector Wolfgang Wilhelm, Count Palatine of the Rhine, c.1614.

EUROPEAN SWORDS

Stephen Bull

Shire Publications Ltd

CONTENTS

Published in 1994 by Shire Publications Ltd, Cromwell House, Church Street, Princes Risborough, Buckinghamshire HP27 9AJ, UK.
Copyright © 1994 by Stephen Bull. First edition 1994. Shire Album 298. ISBN 0 7478 0234 3

Printed in Great Britain by CIT Printing Services, Press Buildings, Merlins Bridge, Haverfordwest, Dyfed SA61 1XF.

Cover: *British infantry officer's sword, pattern 1897.*

British Library Cataloguing in Publication Data: Bull, Stephen. European Swords. – (Shire Albums; No. 298). I. Title. II. Series. 623.4. ISBN 0-7478-0234-3.

ACKNOWLEDGEMENTS
Special thanks are due to David Edge of the Wallace Collection, Colonel J. A. C. Bird (Queen's Lancashire Regiment), Colonel S. M. P. Stewart (Duke of Lancaster's Own Yeomanry), Major D. A. J. Williams (14/20th King's Hussars), Mr J. Blundell (Lancashire County Museums Officer); Mr R. Wilkinson-Latham; also to the photographer, Mike Seed, and Stuart Lloyd. The author is particularly indebted to the late Peter Hayes, formerly Keeper of Weapons, National Army Museum.
Photographs are acknowledged as follows: British Museum, pages 3 (bottom), 4 (both); Colchester and Essex Museum, page 5 (top); Duke of Lancaster's Own Yeomanry, pages 25 (bottom), 29 (top), 30 (bottom); 14th/20th King's Hussars, page 18 (top); Lancashire County Museums, pages 21 (top), 23 (centre); Museum of London, page 3 (top); National Museums of Scotland, page 13 (left and centre); Queen's Lancashire Regiment, page 17; Royal Armouries, pages 11 (left), 14 (left), 16 (right), 28 (left); Turton Tower, page 9 (bottom); the Wallace Collection, pages 1, 6 (both), 7, 8 (top); Robert Wilkinson-Latham, pages 8 (bottom two), 12 (bottom), 20 (all), 21 (bottom), 22 (all), 23 (top), 24 (right), 26 (all), 27 (top and bottom right), 28 (right); York Castle Museum, pages 9 (top), 13 (right).

Parts of a sword hilt: 1, pommel; 2, back strap; 3, guard; 4, grip; 5, ear; 6, ferrule; 7, ricasso; 8, blade; 9, quillon; 10, hilt bar.

Bronze age sword of the typical leaf shape, although this example is rather broader than usual. The hilt would have had grips of bone or wood on each side. Length 62 cm (24¹/₂ inches).

THE FIRST SWORDS

Man's earliest metalwork predates 5000 BC but the first practical swords seem to have evolved during the bronze age three thousand years later. Copper alone was insufficiently tough to make a weapon but an admixture of about 10 per cent tin made it considerably more resilient. Even so axeheads, daggers and arrowheads of metal all predate the sword and were easier to make. Yet by about 1500 BC in Greece the Myceneans were making bronze swords of considerable quality, usually double-edged, and with a tang to which grips of bone or ivory were attached. Many swords have been found in Mycenean shaft graves, some embellished with inlay work and gold.

Soon most of the Greek states were using bronze swords. From the sixth century BC a curved variety became popular both in Greece and Spain. This savage *kopis*, or *falcata*, as it was known in Spain, bears similarities to the modern Gurkha kukri and was primarily a hacking weapon. According to contemporary chroniclers, it was capable of severing an arm at the shoulder with a single blow. The other major sword type of the later bronze age, which was used over a long period, often serving as a sidearm to the hoplite or heavy infantryman, has since been named the *griffzungenschwert* ('grip tongue' sword). In existence by 1000 BC, it was short with a flanged hilt and often had two 'ears' or *antennae* at the top. Similar swords continued in use over much of Europe until at least 400 BC.

After the discovery of iron it was some time before it could be produced to the degree of perfection required for sword manufacture and indeed iron and bronze blades co-existed for about five hundred years. Iron was much harder and was capable of holding a keen edge but it was brittle if cast, and to make a good sword it required forging, hammering and tempering. This last was perhaps the most difficult operation for the hot metal needed to be quenched in oil or water and the wrong temperature could create a weapon too soft to be useful or so hard it would shatter in action.

Two examples of the Spanish 'falcata', c.300 BC. Similar in style to the ancient Greek 'kopis', the 'falcata' was common in the armies of Carthage, whose ranks contained many Spanish troops.

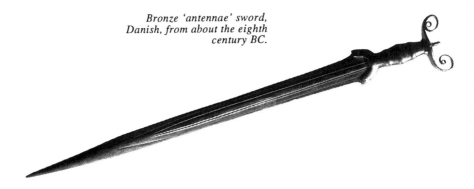

Bronze 'antennae' sword, Danish, from about the eighth century BC.

The Celts were early masters of the fabrication and use of iron swords. The Roman historian Dionysius of Halicarnassus described Celtic warriors whirling their swords above their heads and slashing downwards as though cutting wood. The Romans' best defence was to take such blows on the edge of their shields, which were reinforced with an iron strip. Between 450 and 250 BC the Celtic sword was generally no longer than 65 cm (26 inches) but over the following two centuries they were made progressively larger until a blade 80-90 cm (31-35 inches) in length was normal. They sometimes bear an individual maker's mark.

Roman soldiers were normally armed with the *gladius*, a short broad thrusting sword. The *gladius* apparently originated in Spain and may have first been encountered by the Romans in the hands of their Carthaginian enemies, who employed Spanish mercenaries. The earliest Spanish example has been excavated at Avila and dates to the fourth century BC. Some authors have suggested an even earlier antecedent for the *gladius*, pointing out that its general outline is similar to the weapons of the central European Hallstatt culture, which dates back a further four hundred years.

As the Roman Republic gave way to the Empire and the legions spread out over the known world, their weapons developed and ideas of former enemies were absorbed. The *gladius* generally acquired a narrower blade and instead of tapering

The so-called 'Fulham Sword', a Roman gladius of the first century AD. The decoration of the scabbard suggests that this was once a fine-quality officer's weapon.

4

Tombstone of Marcus Favonius Facilis, centurion of the Twentieth Legion, first half of the first century AD. Note the gladius worn suspended from a belt over the shoulder, with a dagger on the other side of the body. The gladius is found in two main forms, the early 'gladius Hispaniensis', with its gently tapering blade, and the later 'Pompeii' type with parallel-edged blade and short point.

gently to the point had parallel sides for most of its length. The Roman army relied principally on its infantry but towards the end of the Empire in the west and in Byzantium to the east heavy cavalry were becoming more popular. These *cataphracti* adopted a longer cutting sword known as the *spatha* which was like that used by the Celts. With the fall of Rome some tribes continued to use short swords like the *gladius* but soon most had turned to longer weapons. The Franks, for example, favoured a sword with a blade at least 80 cm (31 inches) in length, double-edged and intended for slashing.

The swords of the Dark Ages were expensive and only the rich could afford them. The best were thought to be endowed with mystic qualities and were emblematic of the sovereignty of a lord, the fealty of a warrior and the rites of death. Northern Germany and Scandinavia became centres of manufacture and throughout the Nordic world these arms acquired a certain similarity. Many were buried with their owners, sometimes symbolically broken or bent.

In the boat burial at Sutton Hoo near Woodbridge in Suffolk, which dates to about AD 630, a magnificent sword lay beside its owner. The weapon had been inside a wooden scabbard lined with wool, doubtless selected because the lanolin or natural oils in the wool would keep the blade bright. Radiography demonstrated that the blade was 'pattern-welded' like most swords of the era. This means that several wrought-iron rods or strips had been hammered and twisted together to produce a blade that was resilient and capable of taking a keen edge without brittleness. It is thought that the technique was invented by either the Celts or the Romans. In the Sutton Hoo sword eight bundles of seven thin iron rods had been twisted alternately left and right to create herringbone patterns alternating with parallel lines. Two further strips forged to this core created cutting edges of high-carbon steel, the tempered alloy of iron and carbon. Both the sword and the scabbard were decorated with gold and garnet fittings.

Several swords from the sagas of the Dark Ages bear names. Two such were 'Fishback' and 'Veigarr' – descriptive of a brocaded fabric – and it is likely that these epithets refer to the patterning of the blade. Arthur's 'Excalibur' belongs to a similar era but its description comes to us only through medieval romance. Some of the most spectacular swords came from the boat burials of the ninth and tenth centuries at Hedeby in Denmark. Here guards and pommels are decorated with silver and niello (black silver sulphide), creating images of birds, animals, crosses and interlocking patterns.

5

Two-handed use of a knightly sword.

The hilt of a sword with a 'wheel' shaped pommel, probably French, c.1300. The tang of the sword, which joins the blade and pommel, would originally have been covered with a grip of wood and leather. Notice also the slightly downturned crossguard or quillons.

Early medieval sword types: (left to right) ninth- or tenth-century Scandinavian sword with straight blade and pommel divided into five lobes; French knightly sword, c.1300, with slightly tapering blade and heavy, 'wheel' shaped pommel; German sword with 'Brazil-nut' type pommel, c.1000; sword with flat 'disc' pommel, French or Italian, c.1250.

SWORDS OF THE MIDDLE AGES

The Bayeux Tapestry and other eleventh-century sources show that most swords of the period were long, straight-bladed and with a simple crossguard. Soon, however, a few were to be created which even today impress with their magnificence. Foremost amongst them are the coronation swords of France, Poland and Austria. The French sword, the so-called 'Sword of Charlemagne', probably dates from the twelfth century. The gold hilt and scabbard are set with stones and the quillons are decorated with animal heads. The Polish sword, known as 'Szcerbiec', has been tentatively dated to 1200 and has inscriptions in Latin and Hebrew executed in niello. The Austrian sword was first used at the coronation of Frederick II as Holy Roman Emperor in 1220 and is the plainest of the three. Even so, it is covered in gold enamelling and semi-precious stones.

Despite these flights of fancy, fighting swords remained predominantly simple for most of the middle ages, differing from one another mainly in the shape of the pommel and the angle of the crossguards. One of the pommel variations popular in Germany and central Europe was the flattened 'Brazil-nut' type. Another was the 'disc pommel', round and flat, and apparently widespread, especially in southern Europe. 'Wheel' shaped pommels are also encountered.

Throughout the fourteenth century knightly swords tended to conform to the same general pattern of straight double-edged blade and cruciform hilt but they were often even heavier to combat newly introduced helms and plate armour. Blades were often a metre or more in length, sometimes with a central 'fuller' or groove to lighten the blade, whilst a heavy pommel gave balance. Such swords were often known as 'great' or 'war' swords. An exception to this general description was the 'falchion', a sword with a machete-like blade. This was virtually useless for thrust or parry but could smash through bone and mail like a meat cleaver and even make an impression on plate. Few examples survive although there are a number of artistic representations.

Towards the end of the fourteenth century there began a tendency towards diversification in form and purpose. First

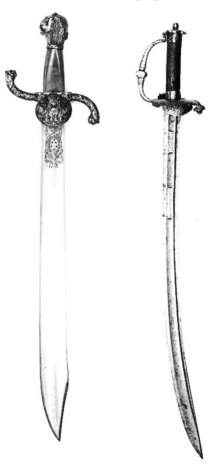

(Left) Italian 'falchion' or broad-bladed sword, mid sixteenth century. The grip is a replacement but the blade shape illustrates a style which had been popular for both war and sport for the preceding two hundred years. (Right) Hunting 'hanger' or short curved sword; English hilt with German blade, c.1640.

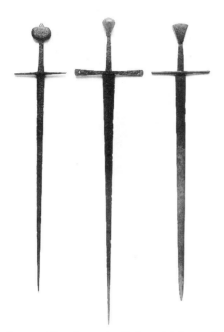

came a number of swords intended for thrusting, with sharply pointed blades of diamond section. Some of these had a blunt portion immediately in front of the grip. Known as the 'ricasso', this allowed the index finger to be placed further forward and gave more control. Elongated pommels permitted two-handed use or a hand to be placed behind the pommel for extra thrust.

In the fifteenth century two further categories of sword appeared in the arsenal – short swords which increasingly supplemented the long knives of the infantry, and fully fledged two-handers. Guards or hilts also became more complicated, both to provide increased protection and to add decoration. At first quillons were simply curved up or down and pommels shaped, perhaps to protect those who did not wear gauntlets. Later a side ring was added to the hilt. These embellishments progressed furthest and fastest in southern Europe and it was from there that the rapier originated in the following century.

Later medieval swords: (left to right) sword with flattened pommel and tapering blade of unknown nationality, c.1380; sword with faceted, fig-shaped pommel and sharply tapering blade, c.1450; sword with triangular flattened pommel and plain quillons, round in section, c.1380.

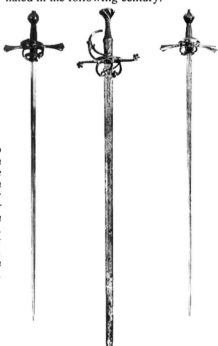

(Left to right) Saxon sword, late sixteenth century; bastard or hand and a half sword, 1540-80; Saxon sword, late sixteenth century.

Saxon rapier with companion 'main gauche', or left-hand dagger, late sixteenth century.

8

Rapier, possibly English, c.1620, with swept steel hilt decorated with a hollow chiselled pommel and wire grip.

THE EARLY MODERN SWORD

During the sixteenth century the rapier developed in a dazzling variety of forms, aided no doubt by the fact that it was often worn by civilians. Sometimes it was seen as a type of male jewellery, pierced, gilded or encrusted with precious stones and with hilt bars bent into elaborate patterns. The rapier was essentially a thrusting sword with a long narrow straight blade; with it developed the art of fencing, the two major schools of fence being the Spanish and Italian. Rapiers were sometimes produced with a matching dagger for the left hand and the pair decorated *en suite*.

Rapier types are so many and complex that they all but defy classification. The most detailed study gives about a hundred basic hilt types and a similar number of pommel shapes. It is, however, possible to list a number of features which aid description and may assist in dating. Simple hilts with a relatively small number of bars tend to be earlier than the more complex types. 'Cup hilts', with their large hemispherical bowl and long quillons to protect the hand, date predominantly from

the period 1630 to 1700, as do those with pierced 'shells'.

At the other end of the scale, two-handed swords of the sixteenth century tended to be simple and massive. Some of the best examples came from southern Germany and Switzerland and were a favoured arm of the Landesknecht mercenaries; they are found with both plain and flamboyant or wavy blades. Other great swords armed the wild men of the Celtic fringe of Europe. The sixteenth-century Irish or Scottish two-hander was the original 'claymore', or *claidheamhmor*, and this term was subsequently, if inaccurately, applied to the basket-hilted broadsword.

'Cup-hilted' rapier, Spanish or Italian, c.1630.

9

Dutch pikeman, c.1600, from Jacob de Gheyn's 'Exercise of Armes'. Notice the rapier worn at a 45 degree angle to the body, suspended by means of a many-looped 'hanger'. The scabbard would almost certainly be of leather but few original examples survive. The metal fittings of the scabbard are the 'chape' at the point and the 'mouthpiece' at the opening.

fan-shaped finials.

During the sixteenth century special swords were evolving for purposes other than war or duelling. Massive broad-bladed blunt-ended executioners' swords are sometimes encountered, for example, but these are much outnumbered by hunting swords. The commonest form of hunting sword was the 'hanger'; these short and curved weapons could be used to finish off a wounded animal or defend the owner in case of extremity. Often they had a simple brass knucklebow and a grip of staghorn, wood or ivory. The finest examples could be richly wrought with precious metals or enamelling and might bear the crest of the nobleman to whose retinue they belonged. Another type of non-military sword which flourished in the sixteenth century was the 'calendar' sword. This was literally a sword with a calendar inscribed upon the blade. Mostly they were intended for hunting and the dates noted may have been thought par-

The true claymore originated about 1500 and could well have a blade exceeding 110 cm (43 inches) in length. Grips were long to accommodate both hands and the quillons often sloped down towards the blade, a feature previously seen on single-handers on tomb effigies of the western Highlands and islands. Some Irish examples have open, ring-shaped pommels and quillons which are terminated in the

Headsman at work with a broad-bladed German double-handed executioner's sword. From Sebastian of Munster's 'Cosmographia', Basle, 1555.

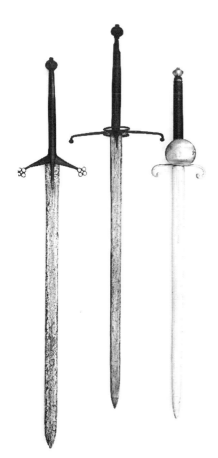

Three claymores. (Left) Scottish or Irish double-hander of the mid sixteenth century with downward sloping quillons and quatrefoil terminals; the maker's mark on the blade, which may be continental, is an orb and cross. (Centre) Scottish claymore of the so-called 'Lowland' style; late sixteenth century. (Right) Early sixteenth-century claymore with 'shell' guards to the hilt, said to have been carried before the Old Pretender when he was proclaimed King in 1715.

Late sixteenth-century 'ribbon' hilted broadsword with long quillons, probably Scottish.

ticularly propitious for the chase. Sometimes the calendars are combined with the signs of the zodiac or other decoration. The fashion for calendar swords continued into the seventeenth century and very occasional examples are found dated as late as 1700.

Special 'boar swords' also first appeared about 1500. The earliest form was simply a very stout-bladed weapon known as the 'estoc' or 'tuck'. These terms were also subsequently applied to forms of cavalry sword. Very soon new versions appeared which were intended to prevent a charging boar getting too close to the huntsman if it became impaled. The main modifications were a broad leaf-shaped tip to

the blade and a crossbar, placed just under it, which would not allow the blade to slip deeper. These features were also found on the contemporary boar spear.

The seventeenth century was notable not only for the final development of the rapier but for the evolution of a number of types of basket-hilted and half-basket swords. Contrary to popular belief, the basket-hilted broadsword was not the exclusive weapon of the Scottish highlander in its early days but was quite frequently made in England and fitted with a German blade. Long-bladed baskets were also associated with the cavalry.

A form of half-basket which is peculiarly English is the so-called 'mortuary'

11

German huntsmen with 'boar' swords. Note the spear points and the stop to prevent the blade penetrating too deeply. From the 'Triumph of Maximilian', 1516.

(Left to right) Italian or German small sword, c.1660; French small sword, c.1660; French small sword, 1660-80.

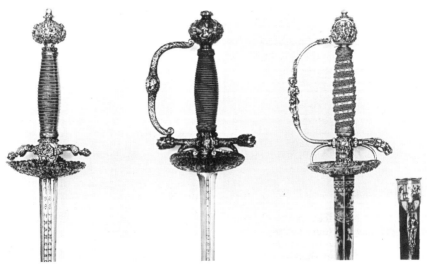

Despite being regarded as archetypically Scottish, many basket-hilted swords are English or have imported blades. (Left to right) Backsword, with one sharpened blade edge and basket hilt, probably English with German blade c.1640. Basket-hilted sword with blade marked 'Andrea Ferrara' but most likely to be German, the hilt by Walter Allan of Stirling c.1735-60. English broadsword with mortuary hilt, decorated with human and animal faces and dolphins. The pommel is of 'lion's head' form, c.1640.

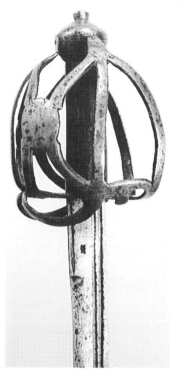

sword. This gets its name from the small faces which are chiselled on the hilt. The Victorians believed that these represented the martyred King Charles I and so 'mortuary' was an apt term. Despite this explanation, many such swords predate the execution in January 1649 and some of the faces are of women. A number of the swords show horsemen or pikemen and even many of the male faces bear little resemblance to Charles. Plainer versions of the mortuary sword, similar in shape but generally having a well-defined shell guard on either side of the blade, are sometimes known as 'proto-mortuary' swords. Despite this name, they probably postdate the original mortuary sword.

Another type of sword, also associated with cavalry, that flourished on the conti-nent at the end of the seventeenth century was the 'schiavona'. Again the hilt was a form of basket and it is thought that the name derives from the Italian word for Slavonic as the Doge of Venice had a corps of Slav bodyguards armed with weapons of this type.

The end of the seventeenth century and the start of the eighteenth were marked by the development of the 'small' sword, which was carried by both officers and civilian gentlemen. As soldiers now relied more on firearms and civilians were expected to have recourse to cold steel only on rare occasions the small sword was, as its name suggests, short, light and compact. Nevertheless it was a mark of status and embellished with engraving, precious metals or stones as the wealth of

13

the owner allowed.

Most small swords have a hilt with a simple knucklebow and a small cup or disc to the front to protect the hand, and a blade of triangular section. Some have what is called a 'Colichemarde' blade, supposedly named after the Swedish soldier John Phillip, Count Von Konigsmark. These blades have a heavy base or 'forte' for parrying but taper suddenly at a shoulder to produce a fine thrusting tip. Many also have hollow faces to the blade flats, making them light but very strong. In the later decades of the eighteenth century small swords continued to be popular but there were new styles of decoration and the blade itself was becoming less practi-

cal. Sometimes the entire hilt was covered in patterns of faceted cut steel studs; sometimes the knucklebow was replaced by a chain. At the end of the eighteenth century the custom of wearing a small sword began to die out amongst most civilians but was retained by some uniformed officials and diplomats.

The 'spadroon' was an essentially naval and military sword which became common in the third quarter of the eighteenth century. The most easily recognised features of the type are the 'stirrup' hilt, the faceted grip, often of ivory or ebony, and the flattened pommel. Sometimes a spadroon would bear a ship's name or a regimental mark.

Left to right: Italian 'schiavona' or broadsword, c.1700. The stamp of the Venetian lion of St Mark appears on the pommel and basket. Broadsword with a cast brass 'shell' guard and a wire grip decorated with classical-style figures, c.1660-70. 'Walloon' hilted sword, c.1660. Distinguished by the pierced discs which form the hilt, the 'Walloon' style sword originated in the Low Countries and became common over much of north-western Europe in the third quarter of the seventeenth century.

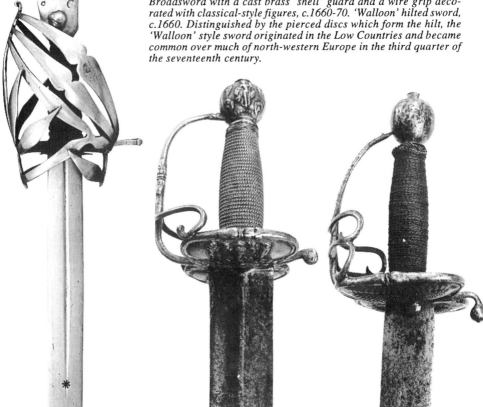

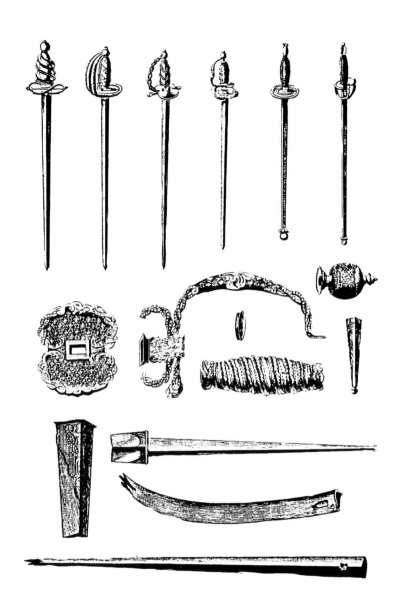

Small swords and their constituent parts from the 'Encyclopedia' of Diderot, c.1761. Top left are four small swords with various hilts; top right are two practice swords, or 'foils', distinguished by the button tips to the blades. Centre is a dismantled hilt showing guard, grip, knucklebow and pommel. Bottom are details of the scabbard and its mouthpiece, and the blade 'tang' which holds together blade, pommel and grip.

Below: *Gold-hilted small sword studded with diamonds, presented by the town of Vittoria to Major General Miguel Ricardo de Alava (1771-1843).*

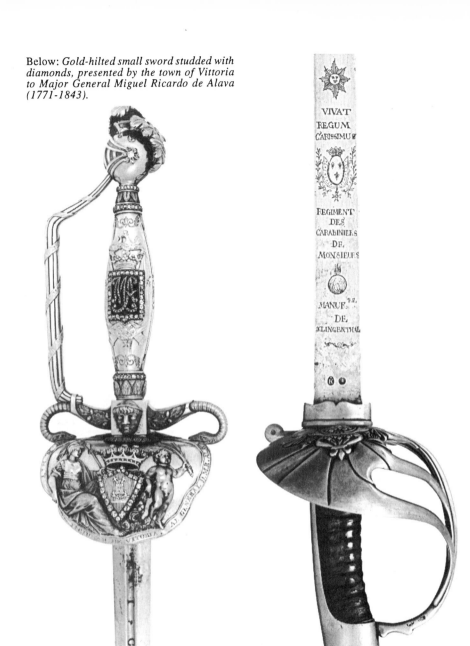

Right: *French carabinier's sword, c.1780, manufactured at Klingenthal.*

Grenadier's brass-hilted 'hanger', third quarter of the eighteenth century. The grip is of shagreen or ray skin and the sword retains the original black leather scabbard with a bar on the mouth for attachment to a frog worn on a belt over the shoulder.

FROM THE LATE EIGHTEENTH CENTURY TO THE PRESENT

During the late eighteenth century both the industrial revolution and improved military administration made their impact on the shape of swords and their production. Several European powers adopted a system of numbering regiments. Previously regiments had been identified by the name of the colonel or of the area from which they came, and a change of leadership or of location meant a change of name. Thus, for example, the Edinburgh Regiment or Leven's Foot now became known as the 25th Foot and the Independent Companies of Invalids became the 41st Foot. New regimental symbols and numbers therefore began to appear on military equipment.

At the same time the equipping of soldiers with edged weapons was progressively taken over from individual colonels by central bodies, and 'patterns' of arms began to be produced which had to be uniform throughout the army. The brass-hilted 'hanger' therefore became the mark of the British infantryman and the *sabre briquet* that of the French. Weapons from all over Europe became covered in 'ordnance marks' as well as the symbols of private makers. These ordnance marks could identify government ownership, like the British broad arrow or the 'BO' of the Board of Ordnance, or they could be the name of an arsenal, such as

Klingenthal of France or Tula of Russia. Such swords were often subjected to a more strenuous testing procedure than their predecessors. British tests took a number of forms and could include measuring and weighing as well as smashing down on a hard surface or sticking in a block and bending.

Cavalry swords were increasingly regularised according to the type of troops for which they were intended. Light cavalry used curved sabres, normally with a simple stirrup hilt, and there is little to distinguish the arm of a French hussar from that of a British or Prussian one. There were, however, two British light cavalry swords of the period, normally identified as the 1788 and 1796 patterns. The former has a brass hilt, the latter steel.

The heavy cavalry used straight or very slightly curved swords, often of the 'Pallasch' style. This had a single-edged, heavy blade, which was used mainly for cutting but was also held straight at the charge. The sword of the French cuirassier was notable for its heavy brass barred hilt and that of the Prussian heavy cavalry for its inclined pistol-type grip. The British 1796 pattern heavy-cavalry sword had a pierced 'disc' hilt and, though vilified for its clumsiness, it could still deliver a shattering blow.

British swords used two major sources

The 14th or Duchess of York's Own Light Dragoons come to blows with French hussars in the Peninsula, c.1813. The British troops are armed with the 1796 pattern light cavalry sword; the French hussar sabre is very similar. Note the use of the sword knot, preventing loss of the sword even when the rider is wounded.

Below: *Cavalry trooper's sword with basket hilt, probably English, c.1760.*

for blades: native examples primarily from Birmingham cutlers, and imported ones from Germany. The latter came mainly from Solingen and many of those used in the Napoleonic era were imported by J. J. Runkel. There was a good deal of discussion as to whether the Birmingham or the Solingen blade was best, and Thomas Gill, a Birmingham maker who claimed some of the most rigorous quality control, marked his blades with the phrase 'Warranted never to fail'. Later, 'proof' marking gained popularity with other makers and many nineteenth-century officers' arms have small round brass inserts in the blades bearing stars, initials or the word 'proof'.

Officers purchased their own swords and these often bear regimental devices or blue and gilt decoration, singling them out as being of better quality than the

Left: *A light dragoon demonstrates the sword-drill 'guard position', with a 1788 pattern light cavalry sword. From 'Rules and Regulations for the Sword Exercise of the Cavalry, 1796'.*
Right: *The 'right give point' position from the 1796 sword drill.*

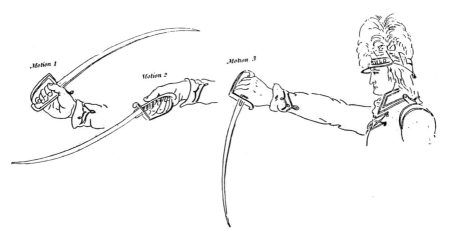

Cut 'number one' as illustrated in the 1796 sword drill. The first motion retires the blade toward the right shoulder 'to gather a sweep', the second is 'the cut', and the third returns the sword to the 'guard' position.

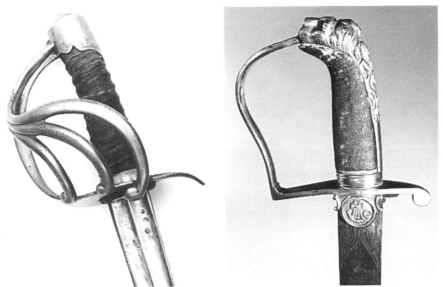

Left: *French cuirassier's sword, model 1801. As with other French edged weapons, the model, date and place of manufacture are engraved on the top flat of the blade.*

Right: *British light infantry officer's sword c.1800: 43rd (Monmouthshire Light Infantry) Regiment; a variation on the 1796 pattern light cavalry sword.*

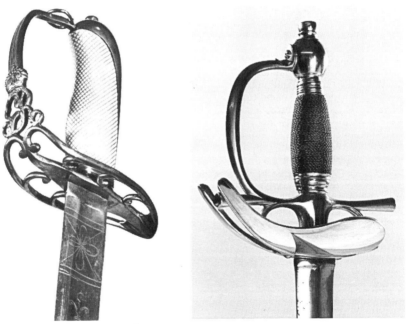

Left: *British general officer's sword, 1803.*
Right: *British household and heavy cavalry officer's sword, 1822 pattern.*

British infantry officer's 1803 pattern sword. Intended for flank company and light infantry officers, the 1803 pattern was also carried by field officers. These swords often vary in detail and certain regiments, amongst them the 52nd and 43rd, adopted different weapons altogether. The guard of this fairly standard example is gilt brass with a lion's head pommel. The blade is blued with gilt decoration.

plain steel of the rankers. Nevertheless, there were also special patterns of sword for officers, such as the 1796 and 1803 patterns of infantry officers' sword, and the 1822 type general officers' sword.

Presentation swords had been given on special occasions for many centuries but their importance grew during the eighteenth and early nineteenth centuries. They were most frequently given as a mark of respect or appreciation by one officer or nobleman to another, or to a ranker for his skill with sword or pistol or for loyal service. Sometimes a town or city would bestow a sword on a general either as a mark of civic respect or to celebrate a victory. Perhaps the best-known of all were the Lloyd's Patriotic Fund presentations given during the Napoleonic Wars from 1803 onwards. These were funded not only by members and insurers at Lloyd's Coffee House but by donations from private individuals, the church and societies. The majority of these were given to naval officers, who were seen as saving Britain's merchant shipping, and thereby the national livelihood, from the French, but a few went to army officers. There were three main grades of Patriotic Fund sword, costing £30, £50 and £100, and a special variation for the victory at Trafalgar.

Few presentation swords were intended for practical use, and most

were worn only on ceremonial occasions, if at all. Even in the twentieth century the presentation of swords has not entirely died out. Perhaps the best-known of modern times was the medieval-style sword presented by Britain to Stalin in the Second World War as a commemoration of the Soviet victory at Stalingrad. Unfortunately, while holding the scabbard Stalin allowed the hilt to dip and the sword slid on to the ground in front of the world's press – a mistake commonly made by those

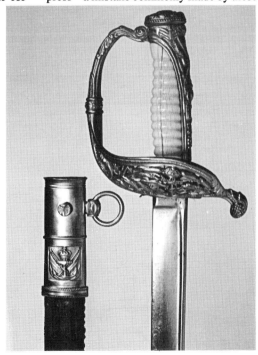

Officer's sword, Royal Netherlands Navy, pattern 1837.

21

Above: *British heavy cavalry officer's sword, pattern 1796.*

Left: *Honourable Artillery Company officer's sword; variation on the 1822 pattern.*

Below: *Lloyd's Patriotic Fund presentation sword.*

inexperienced in handling swords.

In a similar category were dress, levee and court swords worn by soldiers and diplomats. Military dress and levee swords were predominantly light and more decorative versions of practical fighting swords, perhaps with a narrower blade and a decorative inscription. Court and diplomatic swords were essentially descendants of the civilian small sword, marked normally by a royal cipher or monogram.

A hilt which became popular after Napoleon's 1800 campaign in Egypt was the 'Mameluke'. This had a cross hilt and a pistol-like grip turned to one side; there was no knucklebow and the blade sometimes had a stepped or 'latched' back. It was based on the North African and Middle Eastern form known as the 'Shamshir' and its grips were usually of elephant or mammoth ivory. A popular undress sword with officers of the light cavalry, it was much favoured by senior officers and even the Duke of Wellington, a man most unconscious of his accoutrement in the field, owned an example.

Band swords were another area of development in which the result was less than practical, ornate sabres with sharply curved blades and brass hilts being the norm. In the mid nineteenth century British drummers and buglers adopted a very short ornate sword not unlike the *gladius* and usually marked with a regimental distinction or the royal cipher. Drummers usually had brass hilts, buglers silver or white metal.

Blade inscription on a presentation sword of 1821 pattern light-cavalry style given to Sergeant Major Williams as a mark of 'esteem and respect' by Worsley Troop, Duke of Lancaster's Own Yeomanry, 23rd June 1877; made by Mole & Son of Birmingham. Sergeant Richard Hall Williams rode in the Charge of the Light Brigade with the 17th Lancers and the swords carried by the Light Brigade were virtually identical to this one.

Police sword bearing the legend 'Presented to Luke Talbot Esquire Chief Constable of Warrington by the Officers, Sergeants and Constables under his command as a mark of respect and esteem July 29th 1898'; note the black and silver sword knot.

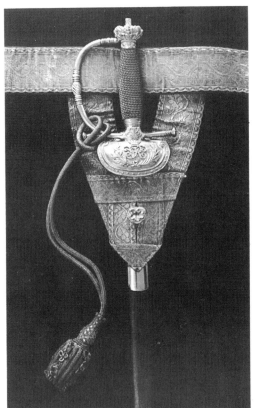
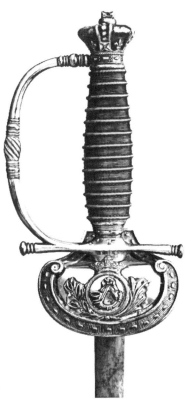

Left: *Victorian Lord Lieutenant's sword, supplied by H. Poole of Saville Row, London. Poole's were at this address from 1867 to 1947; note the original frog and belt with acorn and oak-leaf lace.*
Right: *British sword of a military officer at court, in this case decorated with a light infantry bugle.*

Similar short, classically inspired swords were adopted by military pioneer corps over much of Europe, the Austrians being the first to take up the idea in 1764. Many pioneer swords have a saw back cut into them opposite the blade to enable them to be used as a tool. Russian examples, acquired during the Crimean war, are encountered fairly often in British collections. Britain had begun to introduce short pioneer swords by 1820 but a regulation pattern was not fixed until 1856. This had a brass stirrup guard, a ridged brass grip and a black leather scabbard. It

was not declared obsolete until 1904.

Sword 'knots', lengths of leather or cord that looped around the swordsman's wrist and prevented him losing his weapon in battle, date back a long way but in the late eighteenth and nineteenth centuries they took on a new significance. Knots of different colours or materials were used to denote the bearer's nationality, rank or arm of service. Prussian officers, for example, made extensive use of black and silver braid. British officers used mainly red and gold knots for dress occasions, though there were brown leather 'field

24

Below: *Rifle volunteer officer's dress sword by W. Buckmaster & Company, New Burlington Street, London, c.1870. Like the 1827 pattern regular rifle officer's sword, the hilt cartouche contains a strung bugle; its dress function is betrayed by the narrow decorated blade.*

Above: *1897 pattern sword with steel hilt, 'Presented to Half Squadron Commander J. Prestwich by the National Motor Volunteers (Blackpool Squadron) January 23rd 1917'. The sword was supplied by Fenton Brothers of Sheffield. In the First World War the Motor Volunteers provided transport for the wounded and others within England. The basic sword design was also used by infantry officers.*

Mameluke-hilted light cavalry officer's levee or dress sword with ivory grips and a blade decorated with foliage and trophies of arms; by Garden of London, c.1870.

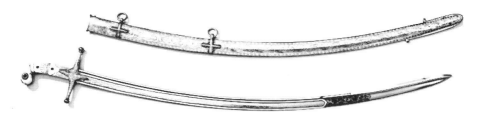

British 15th (King's) Hussars levee sword, c.1870.

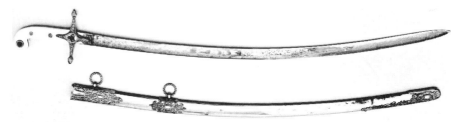

British 18th Hussars officer's levee sword, c.1901.

service' versions. Rifle officers wore a black knot to match their belts and buttons.

From the mid nineteenth century the manufacture of swords became increasingly mechanised. A sword blade began as a steel bar about 30 cm (1 foot) long. This was made red-hot and then drawn out through mechanical hammers and shaped rollers. Next the blade was ground by sandstone wheels, but the finishing was done by hand, excess metal being removed and the final shape being determined by the skill of the grinder.

Next the blade was hardened by heating and quenching in whale oil. During work in the polishing shop blades would not only be polished but would be embellished, principally by acid etching with the aid of wax transfers. The hilt and blade would then be married up and any plating work would take place. It was all an expensive and labour-intensive process, es-

British band sword, c.1820, with lion's head pommel. Often band swords had a chain joining the pommel to the crosspiece in place of a solid knucklebow.

26

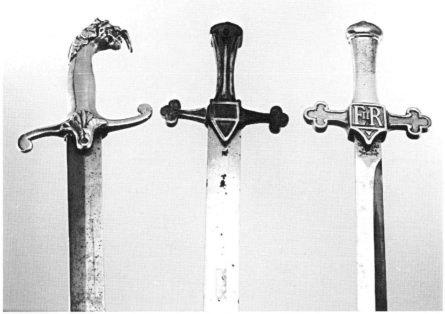

Above: *(Left to right) Band sword, c.1820; drummer's sword, mark I, pattern 1856; drummer's sword, mark II, pattern 1895 (this example c.1960).*

Left: *31st (Oldham) Corps, Lancashire Rifle Volunteers band sword with brass hilt, c.1860. Based on the standard first pattern of the Victorian infantry drummer's sword, the 31st LRV sword is distinguished by the initials on the hilt. More usually a drummer's sword would have a brass hilt and a 'VR' cipher, and a bugler's sword would have a white metal hilt and a bugle.*

Above: *British pioneer sword, c.1830. Pioneer swords were adopted by the Austrians in the eighteenth century, the Prussians about 1810, and by the British and Russians about a decade later. A uniform 'pattern' brass-hilted British pioneer sword was eventually introduced in 1856 and was not declared obsolete until 1904.*

27

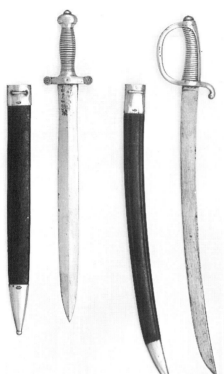

Left: *(Left) The classically inspired French infantry sword, pattern 1831. (Right) French infantry hanger, pattern 1816, made at Klingenthal and dated 1824. The 1831 model was commonly known to the soldiers as 'the cabbage cutter'.*

Below: *Belgian infantry sapper's hanger (Dutch pattern) and naval hanger, c.1880.*

pecially for the best-quality swords for officers. Perhaps the best-known British maker from this period was Wilkinson. The firm had existed since 1772 but achieved pre-eminence in the second half of the nineteenth century. Wilkinson blades for officers' swords bore serial numbers and very extensive records of purchaser and date survive from 1854 onwards. The crossed swords symbol still appears on Wilkinson's shaving equipment.

All this finery and attention to detail obscure the fact that by the nineteenth century all edged weapons were of limited practical use. As firearms became more efficient swords and their accoutrements became steadily more skeuomorphic in their development – features that had once been functional became purely ornamental. Perhaps the last

28

The Duke of Lancaster's Own Yeomanry with drawn swords, c.1895. Notice the buff leather belts in white with matching sword slings and knots.

Charles Melly, captain in the Childwall Rifle Volunteers, c.1865. The sword is a rifle officer's 1827 pattern suspended from a polished leather waist belt.

29

category of swords to retain a practical edge was the cavalry sword. Well-balanced thrusting swords with bowl guards for the hand were usual after 1900 but there were exceptions. Perhaps the best-known is the Russian 'shasqua', a long curved sabre without a knuckleguard, originally the national sword of the Caucasus. It armed not only the Imperial Russian Cossacks but Soviet soldiers after the revolution, suitably emblazoned with a red star. As a strange sop to utility the latest examples were fitted with lugs on the scabbard which allowed the rifle bayonet to be carried.

Even today the sword retains some of its medieval mystique. New officers still buy their own swords on commissioning; swords are still emblematic of civic office or regal power, and they still form a part of the regalia of organisations as diverse as the masonic brotherhood, the Royal Company of Archers and the Royal Navy.

1885 pattern cavalry trooper's sword. This pattern is distinguished by the shape of a Maltese cross cut out in the sheet-steel hilt. This sword was made by Wyersberg & Kischbaum of Solingen and has an issue mark for 1888 together with the marks for a regular dragoon regiment and the Duke of Lancaster's Own Yeomanry.

1912 pattern cavalry officer's sword supplied by Alkit Ltd of Cambridge Circus, London. Note the leather cover sewn over the steel bowl guard, a device often used in India and other sunny places to reduce both glinting and wear and tear.

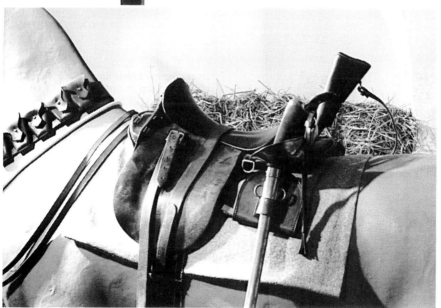

British cavalry furniture, c.1914, showing the mounting of the 1908 pattern bowl-guarded sword. The arched leather container on which the sword rests is for carrying horseshoes.

FURTHER READING

Aylward, J.D. *The Small Sword in England*. Hutchinson, London, 1945.
Blackmore, H. *Hunting Weapons*. Barrie & Jenkins, London, 1971.
Coe, M.D. *(et al)*. *Swords and Hilt Weapons*. Multimedia, London, 1989.
Connelly, P. *Greece and Rome at War*. Macdonald, London, 1981.
Darling, A. *Swords for the Highland Regiments*. Andrew Mowbray Inc, Rhode Island, 1988.
Duffy, A.R. *European Swords and Daggers in the Tower of London*. HMSO, London, 1974.
Hayes-McCoy, G.A. *Sixteenth Century Irish Swords*. National Museum of Ireland, Dublin, undated.
Lenkiewicz, Z. *Marks of European Blade Makers*. Caldra, London, 1991.
May, W.E., and Annis, P.G.W. *Swords for Sea Service* (two volumes). HMSO, London, 1970.
Neumann, G.C. *Weapons of the American Revolution*. Bonanza, New York, 1967.
Newman, P.R. *A Catalogue of the Sword Collection at York Castle Museum*. York Castle Museum, 1985.
Norman, A.V.B. *The Small Sword and Rapier*. Arms and Armour Press, London, 1980.
North, A.R.E. *An Introduction to European Swords*. HMSO, London, 1982.
Oakeshott, R.E. *The Sword in the Age of Chivalry*. Lutterworth, London, 1964.
Oakeshott, R.E. *Records of the Medieval Sword*. Boydell & Brewer, London, 1991.
Robson, B. *Swords of the British Army*. Arms and Armour Press, London, 1975.
Stephens, F.J. *Daggers, Swords and Bayonets of the Third Reich*. Patrick Stephens, London, 1989.
Wallace, J. *Scottish Swords and Dirks*. Arms and Armour Press, London, 1970.
Whitelaw, C.E. *Scottish Arms Makers*. Arms and Armour Press, London, 1977.
Wilkinson-Latham, J. *British Military Swords*. Hutchinson, London, 1966.
Journal of the Arms and Armour Society. London, 1953 to present.

PLACES TO VISIT

Intending visitors are advised to telephone before travelling to find out the times of opening and to check that relevant items are on display.

British Museum, Great Russell Street, London WC1B 3DG. Telephone: 071-636 1555.
County and Regimental Museum, Stanley Street, Preston, Lancashire PR1 4YP. Telephone: 0772 264075.
National Army Museum, Royal Hospital Road, Chelsea, London SW3 4HT. Telephone: 071-730 0717.
Royal Armouries, HM Tower of London, London EC3N 4AB. Telephone: 071-480 6358.
Royal Museum of Scotland, Chambers Street, Edinburgh EH1 1JF. Telephone: 031-225 7534.
Scottish United Services Museum, The Castle, Edinburgh EH1 2NG. Telephone: 031-225 7534.
Victoria and Albert Museum, Cromwell Road, South Kensington, London SW7 2RL. Telephone: 071-938 8500.
York Castle Museum, Tower Street, York YO1 1RY. Telephone: 0904 653611.